THE ART OF DANCE

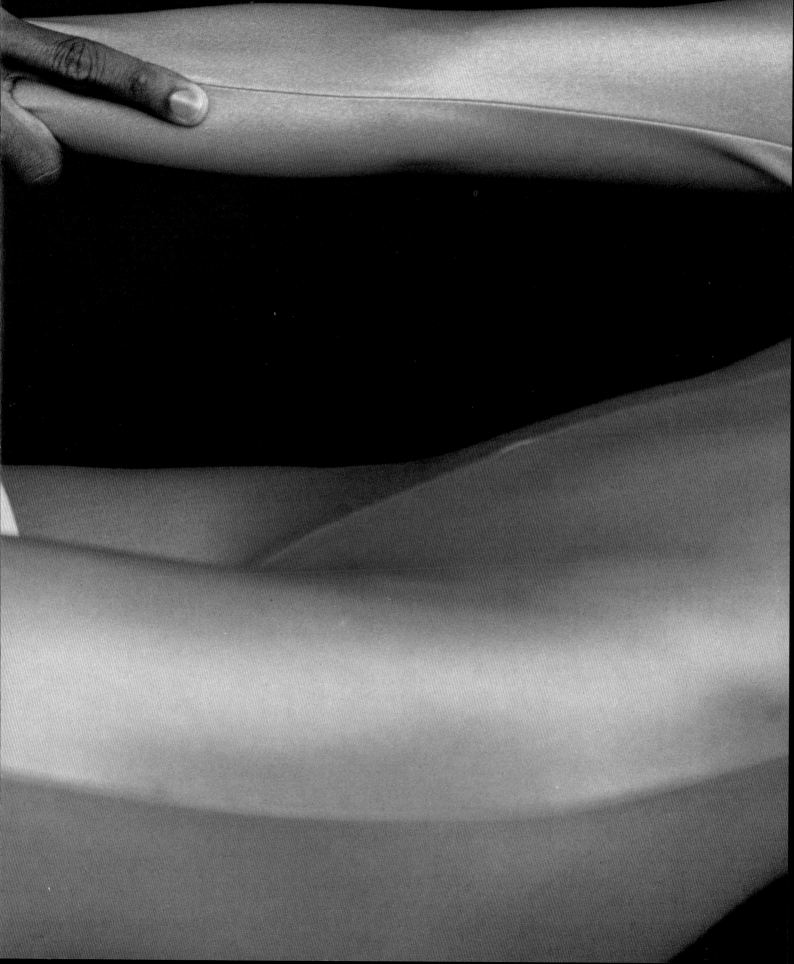

The Art of Dance

HARVEY EDWARDS

Foreword by Bruce Marks

A Bulfinch Press Book
Little, Brown and Company
Boston Toronto London

First Edition

ISBN 0-8212-1734-8

Library of Congress Catalog Card Number 89-43017

Most of the images in this book
were photographed with Nikon cameras and lenses
and film supplied by Agfa.

Bulfinch Press is an imprint and trademark of
Little, Brown and Company (Inc.)

Published simultaneously in Canada by
Little, Brown & Company (Canada) Limited

PRINTED IN SPAIN

To my mother and father, from your world to my world, I love you.

To Eleanor, partner in life, whose love, devotion, great patience and friendship make my work possible. I love you forever.

To Bruce Marks, your genius as dancer, artist, choreographer, artistic director, friend. Thank you.

To Marilyn, from the beginning you believed, supported, and gave me the courage to pursue my dream.

Only God knows how much you mean to me.

To Jennie McGregor, my editor. Although I have tried to capture the essence of dance through my photographs, your words, wisdom, and guidance have brought them into focus.

To Anita Meyer, your poetry and vision have created a bound work of art.

Preface

The world of dance is a magical, mystical one that combines power, energy, and form with the sheer joy of movement. Dance is the culmination of many elements fused together by one prime motivation: expressing emotion.

What drives people to dedicate themselves to a profession that entails grueling work, long hours, physical pain, and the threat that one wrong turn can mean the end of their career? Dancers are special people who commit themselves, both physically and emotionally, to an art form that is of the moment. I try to capture that moment of spatial energy on a frame of film, using light, shading, texture, darkness, lines, space, and my mind's eye.

Watch a train moving over the rails as it goes from one place to another. There is grace and beauty in it. But what makes it all happen? Look at the train from afar, then look closer; look at the engine, closer; the wheels, closer; the gears. Now you can see the beauty, the power of the steel gears, and feel a force of overwhelming energy. This energy is what I try to express through my work. When I attend a performance, my eyes at first see the splendor of the entire stage. When the dancers move, my eyes focus on the energy within their movements. It may be legs entwined or fluid arms lifting a torso high in the air. It may be one long extended leg or the lines of a sweat-drenched neck as I zero in and my emotions take hold. I become captivated and moved at the same time.

My work in dance all began at a gathering of family and friends when I was very young. My cousin Bruce Marks was sixteen at the time. His chiseled features were like a Greek god's. He was a dancer. Everyone in the room was talking about his career and the work it takes to be a dancer, but in my wildest dreams I could not imagine what that meant.

Then someone in the room remarked that his muscles were as strong as steel. This must be a joke, or could the work in dance make his legs like steel? I had to know. Bruce tightened his leg muscle and the reality set in. I could not have imagined that the touch of that iron-like leg would set the course of my life and my love for dance.

Most people see the glitter, glamour, and glitz of the onstage performance. I see the beauty behind the performance, those hundreds of hours in rehearsal for four and a half minutes onstage. To me the real work takes place in the mirror. The awesome reflection of life, both beauty and beast, is there, and the dancer has to harness, tame, and control all that appears within that space of light.

As time moves on while the dancers practice their art, I watch an awkward, uncontrollable form become sleek and sensuous and power-ful. The dancers take on a new light as they develop through the trials and tribulations of each day, working out, perfecting, correcting, and selecting what will be seen in public.

There in the reflected light of the mirror we see the real motivation of a dancer. Expressing joy and sorrow, ecstasy and defeat. I am always in search of dancers to work with, and each one I choose, whether a superstar, in the corps, or taking a class, has the same dedication, drive, and devotion to reaching perfection. In rehearsal, in class, or alone in front of the mirror, the dancer conveys all emotions, and as I watch and try to capture through my lens that beauty of movement, space, and time, I realize why dance is universal and the dancer is the catalyst of life. To express oneself through words takes effort, but to show emotion through movement is a miracle.

Harvey Edwards

9

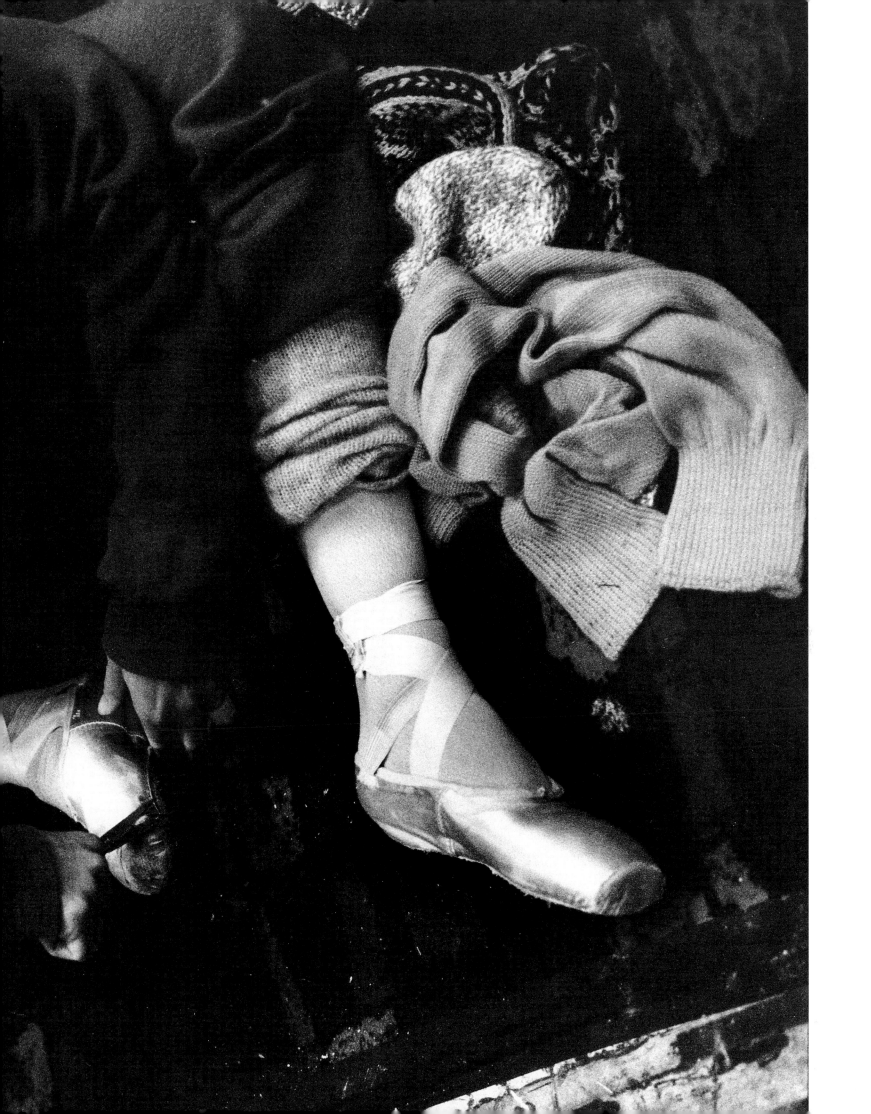

Foreword

Images of dance captured by the lens and transmitted to paper. The power of bodies juxtaposed, ripped leg warmers, worn-out toe shoes, or costumes on a rack next to a touring crate. The eye of Harvey Edwards has selected the world of dance and in so doing has created twentieth-century icons of a universal art form.

My first memories of child Harvey are of his eyes, busy eyes filled with mischief and always occupied . . . eyes that were actively looking. I recall too that at family gatherings he seemed to be everywhere at once and yet on the periphery of the group. I began to detect then what I know now: that he was in the process of placing himself apart. He was creating that distance that the observer/artist must have in order to make an artistic comment. He was, if you will, also asserting his specialness. I could recognize what he was doing. I was doing the same thing.

As I continued my career as a dancer, Harvey and I lost track of each other, or at least I lost track of him: I was and remain the older cousin even though he seems to be catching up. My career was easier to follow since it was documented in the *New York Times*. A Principal Dancer at the Metropolitan Opera, American Ballet Theatre, and The Royal Danish Ballet, I was apparently and without my knowledge providing some inspiration for my father's sister's son.

I began to be aware of Harvey's work at just about the same time as the rest of the world. It was those leg warmers. Does art imitate life or is it the other way around? I was, by then, the Director of Ballet West in Salt Lake City, Utah, and my dancers were all coming to rehearsal in rags. It was, indeed, difficult to see what their legs were doing given the clever camouflage that I will ever attribute to my now no longer long-lost cousin. I was also aware, and jealous, of the beautiful images Edwards had created of Boston Ballet.

In January of 1985 my appointment as Artistic Director of Boston Ballet was announced, and immediately after the press conference I called Harvey. He was, of course, shocked to hear from me after a quarter of a century and even more surprised that I was now the director of his "favorite" company.

Since our reunion we have become family again, and Harvey, Eleanor, and children have moved to Massachusetts. I am proud to claim him, and in turn he has claimed me as "his way into dance," his inspiration. I'm not sure that that is true, but I do know that it feels wonderful to have him nearby, to work with him, and to laugh with him. I am proud to introduce his work to you.

Bruce Marks   Artistic Director, Boston Ballet   13

Harvey Edwards is a superb magician whose camera makes the beauty and power of dance come startlingly alive.

Alvin Ailey

Artistic Director, The Alvin Ailey American Dance Theater

Warm-up/Classes/Practice

Once I became a professional dancer there was no return. The excitement and mystery of the theatre had captured me forever. The art of dancing for me now is from the rehearsal studio to the stage. The creative process felt here during our daily work in the studio continually helps me to grow. Through performing a variety of ballets and meeting the demands of their individual roles, I mature as an artist.

Denise Pons
Soloist
Boston Ballet

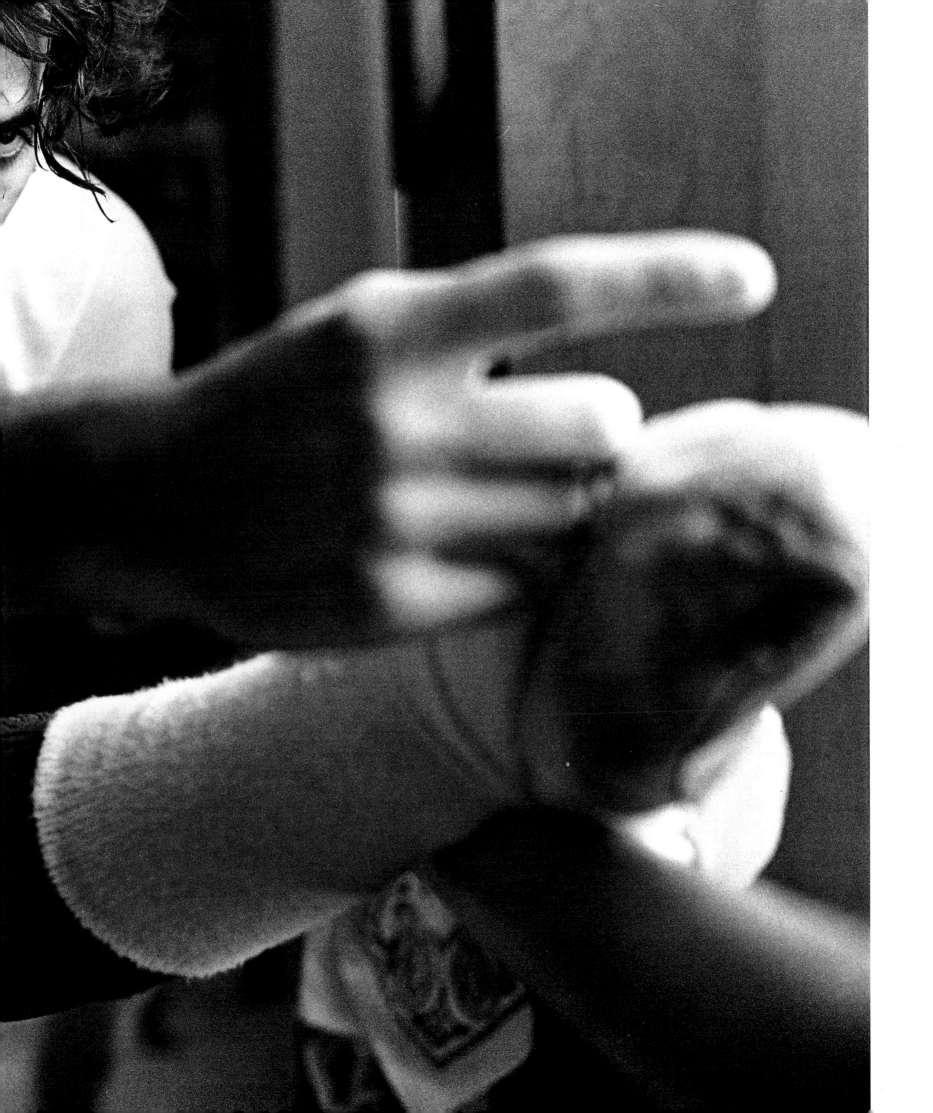

38

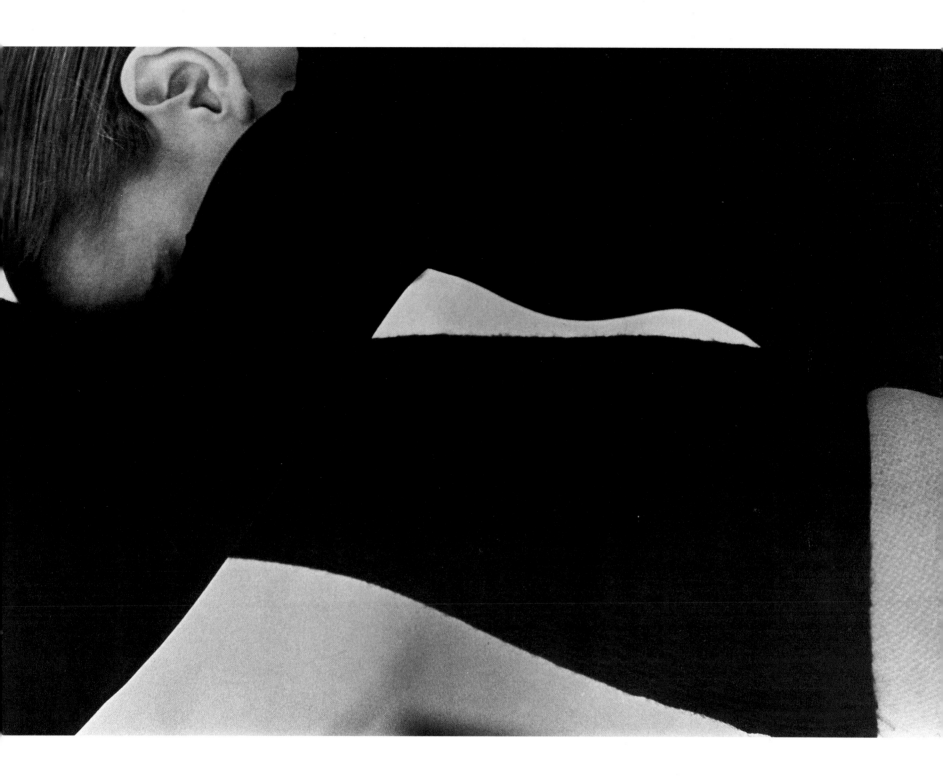

To dance is to feel the breath of
life flowing through the soul and
creating harmony with the music.
Once the torment and ecstasy
come together, dance—magic—
is created onstage or in the studio.

What quality inspires the dancer,
what passion impels the young
dancer to create? How magnifi-
cent is this creativity when given
the chance to flourish, when the
talented dancer is allowed to grow
as an artist.

Oh, the glory of ballet! What is
it about ballet that sets it apart
from all other forms of movement?
Is it the music, the costumes, the
line and fluidity of the dancers, or
is it the purity and elegance of the
art itself? It is all of these and
something more. Without the glitter, sans costumes, even on a
barren stage, even in rehearsal
clothes, ballet remains the most
enchanting form of dance ever
created.

Edith D'Addario
Executive Director
Joffrey Ballet School

Forms/Positions/Images

How do I love dance?

Artistry.

Reverence for Pavlova.

Veneration for Balanchine.

Enlightenment of young dancers.

Yes, I love to dance!

Every day I try harder.

Did I make the right choice?

Why do I dance?

Applause?

Reviews?

Destiny!

Elaine Bauer

Principal

Boston Ballet

Dance is an art form that is dedication and work. It takes many years of training to make it look effortless. Many photographers have been influenced by the lines that a dance artist makes.

Photographs give us an opportunity to see certain positions and poses differently. By changing an angle, or going close up, in a totally different position, we can see a different aspect of the set pose.

Eddie J. Shellman   Principal, Dance Theater of Harlem

A new ballet is a step into the unknown, a trip into the fourth dimension of one's self. It is an artistic endeavor using God's highest creation as the medium. On with the dance!

Gerald Arpino
Artistic Director
The Joffrey Ballet

120

In my opinion, dance is one of the most complete visual arts.
It is through dance that we create illusions that we try to sustain for the longest possible moment.

Fernando Bujones   Principal/Guest Artist

Edited by Jennie McGregor

Designed by Anita Meyer, Boston

Copyedited by Peggy Freudenthal

Production coordinated by Amanda Wicks Freymann

Type set in Syntax and Bauer Bodoni by Monotype Composition Company, Boston

Color separations by Reprocolor Llovet, Barcelona

Printed and bound by Cayfosa, Barcelona